A Sacred Way
to
Gain Freedom
from
Multi-Generational
Curses

ELIZABETH GRIEST

Inks and Bindings
888-290-5218
www.inksandbindings.com
orders@inksandbindings.com

Contents

Dear Reader,

For decades, I've suffered from Multi Generational Curses.

Healing Freedom is a Process for me, as I believe it is for others so afflicted.

May this Sacred Way help you as much as It is helping me.

Prayers/Blessings,

Elizabeth Griest

I

Multi Generational Curses have plagued me for decades – at times more so, than at other periods.

Curse Causes? I'm still learning; but, the roots are separation from God; separation from myself; separation from caring others.

Such separation can result in <u>un</u>wise choices; distorted thinking; poor communication with oneself especially with one's Inner Child; poor communication with others.

These are all symptoms of Soul Sickness.

_____

_____

_____

_____

_____

_____

_____

_____

_____

_____

_____

II

I find it's usually more helpful/healing for me to focus more upon Sacred Solutions rather than Curse Causes.

Though at times it truly is necessary to clearly see Causes.

_____

_____

_____

_____

_____

_____

_____

_____

_____

_____

_____

_____

_____

_____

_____

_____

III

It's Essential for me to remind my Inner Child and myself Gaining Healing Freedom is a Process. And, sometimes is slower than she/I desire.

_____

_____

_____

_____

_____

_____

_____

_____

_____

_____

_____

_____

_____

_____

_____

_____

_____

_____

_____

IV

The Inner Child contains one's deepest feelings, memories, beliefs about oneself, others, life, God.

The Inner Child also holds the Blue Print of one's Divine Destiny – that which one arrived on Earth to live/do which is Universal, yet, Individualized.

Universal in that we are all to Grow in Empathy and Prayer for ourselves and others.

Individualized in that we all have a Sacred Life Plan that is Uniquely our own.

_____
_____
_____
_____
_____
_____
_____
_____
_____
_____
_____
_____
_____
_____
_____

V

One's Sacred Life Purpose can be disrupted—even nearly destroyed by Multi Generational Curses.

_____

_____

_____

_____

_____

_____

_____

_____

_____

_____

_____

_____

_____

_____

_____

_____

_____

_____

_____

_____

_____

VI

Multi Generational Curses were highly Instrumental in lifelong poor health – even my near death.

VII

Multi Generational Curses were highly Instrumental in my decades of living at the poverty level or below.

_____

_____

_____

_____

_____

_____

_____

_____

_____

_____

_____

_____

_____

_____

_____

_____

_____

_____

_____

_____

_____

VIII

Multi Generational Curses were highly Instrumental in various troubles I experienced with some women and some men.

Especially with men.

_____

_____

_____

_____

_____

_____

_____

_____

_____

_____

_____

_____

_____

_____

_____

_____

_____

_____

_____

IX

Now, I must express the most gut and heart wrenching component of my Multi Generational Curses.

Namely, the Incubus – an evil entity – a disembodied male – who victimizes human females.

An Incubus's wicked female counterpart is a Succubus who preys upon human males.

_____

_____

_____

_____

_____

_____

_____

_____

_____

_____

_____

_____

_____

_____

_____

_____

X

Both Foul Beings demonstrate powerful sexual exploitation of their human targets.

XI

Both Wicked Entities abuse their human victims in additional ways other than erotically.

XII

⚜

These Evil Entities essentially have one aim – to
dominate and destroy their human targets.

XIII

In my case, the Incubus desired to drive me mad then have me suicide.

_____

_____

_____

_____

_____

_____

_____

_____

_____

_____

_____

_____

_____

_____

_____

_____

_____

_____

_____

_____

_____

_____

XIV

---·❖·≫≪·❖·---

The Incubus strives to cause me to make bad choices regarding my health, my safety, my security, my finances, all my relationships – though, especially with men.

_____

_____

_____

_____

_____

_____

_____

_____

_____

_____

_____

_____

_____

_____

_____

_____

_____

_____

_____

_____

XV

The Incubus desires me to never know/live my Sacred Life Purpose.

_____

_____

_____

_____

_____

_____

_____

_____

_____

_____

_____

_____

_____

_____

_____

_____

_____

_____

_____

_____

_____

XVI

The Incubus capitalizes on fear, sadness, resentment, guilt, shame.

XVII

Particularly my Inner Child has been the hardest hit by the Incubus's attacks.

_____

_____

_____

_____

_____

_____

_____

_____

_____

_____

_____

_____

_____

_____

_____

_____

_____

_____

_____

_____

_____

_____

XVIII

Shame is the Incubus's most brutal weapon aimed at my Inner Child.

XIX

❖

Shame differentiates from guilt in that guilt says
I made a mistake. Shame declares I am a mistake.

_____

_____

_____

_____

_____

_____

_____

_____

_____

_____

_____

_____

_____

_____

_____

_____

_____

_____

_____

_____

XX

My Inner Child was bombarded by others with a slew of Shaming statements about my illnesses, my fears, etc.

My Inner Child carried such Shaming statements from previous lives, also.

_____

_____

_____

_____

_____

_____

_____

_____

_____

_____

_____

_____

_____

_____

_____

_____

_____

_____

XXI

Unfortunately, in this life as a child I also experienced, plus witnessed some sexual brutality.

Later, as an adult in this life the pattern was repeated.

Therefore, the Shame Spiral/Cycle continued because always I partly felt I was to blame. I was inherently defective, thereby deserving of such brutalities.

_____

_____

_____

_____

_____

_____

_____

_____

_____

_____

_____

_____

_____

_____

XXII

Thus, the Incubus greatly drew upon and magnified my deeply rooted intense shame.

XXIII

As with all my Multi Generational Curses my Inner Child/I need to grow in Empathy and Prayer for myself; offenders; shamers/blamers; ancestors.

My Child Self/I also need to grow in Sacred Release of the Multi Generational Curses and their myriad miseries.

Plus! My Inner Child/I need to grow in Sacred Release for myself; offenders; shamers/blamers; ancestors.

_____

_____

_____

_____

_____

_____

_____

_____

_____

_____

_____

_____

XXIV

As tough as it can be – and often is – my Inner Child/I need to grow in Empathy and Prayer for even the Incubus.

Such Empathy and Prayer recognizes the torments all such demonically driven entities experience. However! Such Empathy and Prayer does <u>NOT</u> condone the entities' actions.

As tough as it can be – and often is – my Child Self/I need to grow in asking for Sacred Release for all tormentors so that they can Experience Sacred Parents of All's Healing Grace and Mercy.

And! So that <u>all</u> torments <u>cease</u> for everyone.

_____

_____

_____

_____

_____

_____

_____

_____

_____

_____

_____

XXV

My Inner Child/I need especially to say Prayers of Empathy as well as Prayers of Sacred Release for our ancestor who sold his soul to the Prince of Darkness, thereby resulting in the Incubus.

Said ancestor made his <u>Un</u>holy Pact to gain wealth and power.

Very likely my ancestor's Inner Child was craving security and importance.

_____

_____

_____

_____

_____

_____

_____

_____

_____

_____

_____

_____

_____

_____

XXVI

It's Essential for my Inner Child/I to continue growing in a Healing Relationship with myself/ others/ Sacred Mother/Father God of All.

_____

_____

_____

_____

_____

_____

_____

_____

_____

_____

_____

_____

_____

_____

_____

_____

_____

_____

_____

_____

_____

_____

XXVII

❖·❀·❀·❖

As a mystic and author, it's Essential for my Child Self/I to persistently grow in Sacred Union with myself/ others/ Sacred Mother/ Father God of All.

_____
_____
_____
_____
_____
_____
_____
_____
_____
_____
_____
_____
_____
_____
_____
_____
_____
_____
_____
_____
_____

www.ingramcontent.com/pod-product-compliance
Lightning Source LLC
Chambersburg PA
CBHW020348130626
46549CB00003B/1356